WILBERT BLACK

INVEST IN REAL ESTATE

The Ultimate Guide on How to Make Money in Real Estate,
Discover Expert Advice and Useful Tips on How You Can
Make Money By Investing in Real Estate

Descrierea CIP a Bibliotecii Naţionale a României
WILBERT BLACK
 **INVEST IN REAL ESTATE. The Ultimate Guide on How
to Make Money in Real Estate, Discover Expert Advice and
Useful Tips on How You Can Make Money By Investing in Real
Estate** / Wilbert Black. – Bucharest: Editura My Ebook, 2020
 ISBN

WILBERT BLACK

INVEST IN REAL ESTATE

The Ultimate Guide on How to Make Money in Real Estate, Discover Expert Advice and Useful Tips on How You Can Make Money By Investing in Real Estate

My Ebook Publishing House
Bucharest, 2020

TABLE OF CONTENTS

INTRODUCTION

Real Estate investing is one of the most simplistic ways to earn money. With a relatively small monetary investment and some sweat equity, you can turn a substantial profit. The future outlook on real estate investing is positive and constantly evolving.

For new investors, one of the most difficult hurdles to overcome is learning the ropes of the real estate business. Real estate transactions are complicated, and if you are not educated on the ins and outs of the business, you potentially could lose large amounts of money, fast.

Before you get started in real estate investing, spend some time thinking about the best approach for your financial situation, personality, and risk tolerance.

One in four residential homes is bought as investment property. Many real estate investors are regular people just like you who make impressive side incomes.

Some people even earn enough to make real estate investing their primary income.

In this book, you'll learn about strategies you can use when investing in real estate, the nuances of the complicated sales process, and other points to consider – like real estate law, tax implications, and non-traditional real estate investment options. While being a real estate investor is, at times, stressful, it also can be mentally and financially rewarding.

CHAPTER 1

STRATEGIES IN REAL ESTATE INVESTING

Is Real Estate Investing for You?

Real estate is an intricate business that involves many different legal, financial, and interpersonal aspects. Are you ready to jump into this complicated business? Think about these essential questions before you make your first move.

1. How much money can you invest?

Investing in the real estate market requires capital. The initial outlay of cash needed upfront to acquire a property may be large or small. However, once you assume ownership of the property, you are legally responsible for the full loan amount. Be sure you can afford to invest by looking closely at your personal financial situation. How much cash do you have? What amount of debt and how much interest can your finances handle? Think about how much you can lose.

2. Are you risk tolerant?

Risk and capital go hand-in-hand. How much risk are you comfortable taking on? A large loss to a small investor has a much larger impact than the same amount to a wealthy investor with deep pockets. While risk-taking can be exhilarating, be honest about your finances and think about the level of risk that will be comfortable to you. Do you naturally enjoy taking chances, or do you tend to be more risk adverse? It's essential to success to know your comfort zone.

3. What are your future financial plans?

Are you interested in investing to maintain capital or to get the highest return in the shortest amount of time? Consider the amount of time, money, and risk associated with each scenario. Be logical. A straight 15% profit over a couple of weeks is not realistic. If you are interested in a high return, this usually means there's a longer time commitment, which means your money will be tied up. The value of property can change quickly, leaving you in a higher risk situation.

4. Do you have what it takes?

To be successful in real estate investing, you need to be detail oriented, a quick learner, and have excellent interpersonal skills. You need to have the self-management skills required to determine what you need to know, then go out and learn it and apply it.

5. How much time can you spend?

Think carefully about how much time you can commit to the day-to-day tasks required to be successful in this business. In the beginning, you'll need to spend a lot of time researching and learning about the business. With every endeavor you'll need to spend time working on legal issues, zoning and town issues, insurance, tax concerns, contracts, market research, financing.

If after considering these questions you are still interested in real estate investment – congratulations! This field is one of the most exhilarating ways to make a living.

Your First Real Estate Investment

Making your first real estate transaction, either as your primary residence or as a planned investment, can be profitable and exciting, but it can be overwhelming too. Follow these steps when starting out in real estate investing.

1. *Educate yourself.* This doesn't mean that you need to go back to school, but you do need to take responsibility for what you need to know, and learn it. Study the market you're interested in entering. Use the internet, local land records, and area real estate agents to find the sales prices of comparable properties. Learn about the transaction process, each person's role and responsibility, the legal requirements, and insurance. Each component carries fees that vary, and by researching prices you can avoid losing money.

2. *Get your financing in order.* A common mistake made by first time investors is to find the property first, then get financing. Before you go out to find that hidden gem, get pre-approved for financing. Decide on a lender by choosing a bank, mortgage company or online loan company. When talking with your lender, tell them how much you are looking to invest. They'll gather lots of financial information about you – income, credit history, liabilities – and give you an idea of how much they'll finance. With the many different financing choices available today, you'll need to decide which option works best for you. Financing plans have different variables including different rates, initial cash investment, and tax implications.

12

3. *Look for your property*. Finding real estate that you can make a profit with can be tricky. Use the internet and local newspaper's "Real Estate" section. Look for abandoned and "For Rent" homes. Drive around the area you're interested in and try to find "For Sale by Owner" properties.

4. *Negotiate a fair deal.* Once you've found the perfect house, you'll need to negotiate for the best price. Don't expect that you'll get a steal. Sellers are trying to the most money for their property, and buyers are trying to pay the least amount. Negotiating well involves working together with the seller to find a win-win situation. Be assertive, but plan to make concessions. Inflexibility often causes expensive delays and added stress.

Profiting in Real Estate

One report indicates that over 23% of total home sales in 2004 were bought as investment properties. This is not a surprise, since home prices have had a high percentage increase in recent years and the market has been experiencing high returns.

There are many ways to make money investing in real estate. "Flipping" a property means that you buy it, fix it up quickly, and resell it for a profit.

Foreclosures are another way to get investment property, which is when a home owner defaults on a loan and the mortgage holder then puts it up for auction.

With abandon property, it's often unclear who holds the title to the property, so there's extensive title research and legal work that occurs with these properties. Paper investments, or non-property real estate investments, are when you invest in a mutual funds or bond that is directly related to the real estate market, but not actual property. These investments should be made with advice of a professional broker.

Manage Your Exposure

Managing the risk associated with investing in real estate is key to protecting yourself from loss. The most important aspect of risk management in real estate is to know the law. It's essential that you have a working knowledge of the real estate legal structure and requirements.

After you've researched property availability, cost, and buyer interest, you'll need to hypothesize about what the future holds for your market. Will prices go up or down?

When considering your risk, keep the following points in mind:

1. *Think about the local economy.* Are there jobs available or are most companies in the area losing jobs? Are new homes being built more or less than over the past 5 years?

2. *Make wise financing choices.* When picking your funding source, think about how long you plan to keep the property. Adjustable Rate Mortgages (ARMs) are attractive because of their lower down payments and lower rates. You can pick the duration of the loan – typically either 1,5, or 7 year ARMs – and your rate will be adjusted to the prevailing rates after this period of time. If you plan to hold onto a property longer than the ARM, ARMs can cost you more because of the higher interest rates. It may be more prudent to opt for a fixed rate mortgage with the shortest length you can handle financially.

3. *Pay a large down payment to reduce your risk.* If you can put down 10%, you'll have instant equity in the property, and most likely get a better interest rate.

4. *Be creative with your mortgage payments.* Make larger monthly payments then require, or make one extra payment a year you'll reduce your principle.

Getting the Highest Return

To make the most money possible in real estate, the standard philosophy is to "buy low, sell high". Most people try to do this, and many do not succeed because it's hard to do. When trying to get the highest return possible, keep your costs down and do everything possible to draw in the highest bidders.

Once you own the property, do as much of the repair work yourself, as long as it is of a professional level. Shoddy work and inferior materials will cost more to correct later. With difficult projects, hire a trained professional from a small scale operation. Large contractors with several employees have to factor their large overhead into their prices.

When looking to maximize your profits, try to save money with your lender. Look around for cheaper loans with the less popular lenders. The large banks and financing companies usually have high fees and rates. Don't accept overpriced fees. For example, your lender is charging $75 to deliver a few papers a short distance, ask for it to be reduced.

By educating yourself on the legal and accounting aspects of real estate transactions, you can save yourself thousands of dollars. If you learn the basics of these two areas you will know when to ask for a professional's help.

When negotiating, be firm but flexible. Attempt to find a win-win situation where both you and the other party walk away from the table happy. Be clear on what you want, and what you can be flexible on. If the other party walks away angry and feeling cheated, they might try to sabotage your attempt to make a profit.

If you are selling your property, it's important to also shop around and negotiate for the best prices on high priced items, real estate commissions, and closing costs.

"Staging" is setting the scene by making your property look its best. You will get the highest price for a property that has been properly prepared.

Actively market your property and you'll get the largest pool of potential buyers possible. It is a benefit to the seller if there are several interested parties in your property.

Buy and Sell at the Right Time

Timing is important in all investments, but unlike other investments – bonds, stocks, and mutual funds to name a few - there are two characteristics specific to real estate investing.

1. Real estate transactions take a long time.
2. Each piece of real estate is unique.

In order to buy or sell property it takes a long time, and while the transaction is taking place, the market is constantly changing. This makes timing the purchase or sale of real estate tricky. When you are investing in real estate, you are trying to sell high and then jump back into the market by buying low. Timing the market in such a way is a challenge.

Look for property that is a "fixer upper" to get a good deal. If you have an aptitude for home repair or you know an inexpensive worker, you can increase the value of a home by over 10%. Search for foreclosure auctions and Notice of Default alerts in the area newspapers and online. Find a good deal on property by anticipating positive change in depressed areas. Up-and-coming neighborhoods, in areas where people have been leaving tend to have lower prices. Find areas where the government is involved in development efforts.

The key to employing any of these strategies is the access to capital. This doesn't mean having an account with a large sum of money in it. Instead, you need to have access to money. By maintaining a high credit score, nurturing an efficient relationship with your lender for quick approval for financing, and having access to liquid assets, you'll be prepared to jump when the right deal comes along.

Even in a slow market, the chance to make a profit investing in real estate is still likely. To do this, however, you'll need to do your homework, have a long-term outlook, and be able to walk away from any deal.

Saving Cash on Little Things Adds Up

Buying property is one of the largest purchases you'll ever make. Even if you aren't putting up a large down payment, by having a mortgage you are making yourself responsible for a sizable amount of money. There's also the possibility of tax consequences.

By saving as much cash as you can, you'll have money for the things that inevitably pop up. As it is, you know you'll need to pay for the closing costs and the initial down payment.

Closing costs include the mortgage, fire and hazard insurance, title fees, and many other costly items.

Follow these tips to save money:

1. Get the best financing deal you can find. First and foremost, be sure to have your financing in place BEFORE you make an offer. To get the best deal, research the rates available for your credit score and try to get financing companies to compete for your business. Ask what options are available given your credit rating. Negotiate with your lender to lower or

eliminate costly fees and charges. Avoid paying an application fee if you can.

2. Find your own providers. You don't have to use the companies that your agent or lender recommend. This is important when selecting your title and insurance company. Your agent and lender have lists of recommended companies because they have pre-established relationships. Keep in mind that you are the one paying them. Carefully review their fees and rates before making a decision. You can use any company you wish.

3. Be willing to negotiate. Even a seller in a seller's market needs to be flexible. People sell for many reasons – death in the family, divorce, job transfers, etc. Sellers in these situations are highly motivated to complete the real estate transaction quickly at almost any cost. If you're willing to work with them and be flexible, you may get a good deal.

TIP:

Consider negotiating a deal where the seller pays a larger portion, or all, of the closing costs.

CHAPTER 2

THE REAL ESTATE SALES PROCESS

All About Flipping

Buying real estate and selling it again fast, and ideally for a profit, is called "flipping". This type of real estate investing is completely legal and ethical. Negative press over flipping real estate probably comes from media coverage of real estate fraud situations, where people have intentionally overpriced the market value of a home, fraudulently completed documents, or worked with others to take advantage of a buyer. None of this happens in an honest flip.

Finding a property that is a good flip requires a few ambitious steps on your part. You'll be looking, most likely, for an under priced home in need of repair. Or you will be looking for a seller that wants to sell fast, thus getting you a lower price.

One way to find property leads is to talk to friends, family, business associates, real estate agents, or bankers. Go out to the neighborhood you're considering and look for "For Sale by Owner" signs, or ring doorbells to see if anyone in the area is considering selling.

Check the public land records and look for "fire sales". This usually means that the owner of the property is having difficulty making mortgage payments. If you contact them and they agree to sell, you're helping them out of their difficult financial situation. And you're getting a property that may make a profit. If done respectfully, there's nothing unethical about this transaction.

To be a successful real estate flipper, you will need to hone or develop many skills. You will need to have an eye for the diamond in the rough. You should be able to accurately size up buyers. It is best if you are handy and can take care of basic home repairs. It is very important that you are detail oriented and a multi- tasking project manager. Flipping involves many details, and it's important to be on schedule with the project to avoid costly delays. Lastly, you will need to have superior interpersonal skills.

Plan to retain the services of a professional accountant, unless you are sufficient at these skills. Also find a good lawyer who can provide you with legal counsel.

Finding Financing – Creative Ideas

For many years, the way to finance real estate was to make a 20% down payment, and get a loan for the remaining 80%. Of course you could make a higher down payment, but 20% was typically the minimum. Luckily, this standard has changed.

There are now several finance options available to the real estate investor. One popular way to finance your purchase is to have a second mortgage. The buyer makes a 5% down payment, and borrows the remaining 15%, usually at a higher interest rate, on a different loan.

Even though it's nice to invest less on a property, the higher interest rate isn't the only drawback. Usually, if the buyer does not meet the 20% minimum, they are required to get costly private mortgage insurance (PMI).

You are able to remove PMI when the loan-to-value (LTV) ratio reaches 80%. This is achieved by paying down the second mortgage and appreciation of the property value. This does not happen often because the property is usually sold or the buyer refinances before PMI can be removed.

23

For creative investors, other financing sources exist. Manufacturers of homes in planned developments are often willing to provide financing to early buyers.

Another risky and rather complicated way of financing a property is called 'sub2' which stands for 'subject-to'. This type of deal is when the seller gives you the deed to the property, the loan stays in place, but the buyer never legally takes over the loan, just the payments. There are many different versions of this kind of transaction. Because of the complexity and risk, this method of funding an investment is not recommended for beginners.

You can also consider forming a limited partnership to finance your real estate investment. There are many different arrangements on this method. Some types involve each person in the partnership contributing in a portion of the cost, usually 50% each. However, sometimes the profit is distributed relative to the original amount invested. Another arrangement is that one half of the partnership contributes the capital, and the other half provides the needed services, such as repairs on a home that needs to be fixed. There are many different variations of this method.

Government loans are available to low income investors, or buyers who have served in the military. These programs are usually only available for primary residences.

Did you ever think about buying a home on a credit card? This is another method of financing your real estate purchase, although it's usually not recommended. Obviously, the interest rates on most credit cards are substantially higher than loan rates. Another drawback is that lenders determine your creditworthiness based on your outstanding debt, and if you use credit card cash advances to cover the 5-20% down payment that you need, you'll probably get turned down for a loan. This is also true for money borrowed from friends or family, unless you can show that the money is truly a gift.

The Lender's Perspective on Loaning Money

Lenders are in the business of lending people money because they make carefully calculated decisions based on your risk. They have two expectations; that you will repay them and that they will make a profit. To judge if you are capable of meeting those two criteria, lenders look closely at your current financial position and your historical financial situation.

When judging your financial past, lenders will look at:

1. *Credit history*. They'll review the size and number of previous loans and the repayment history on those loans. They'll also look at your FICO scores and various other raw data.

2. *Income history*. What is your profit history on your other investments? Over what length of time? They'll look at the last three years of income statements and tax returns, your debt, and any legal judgments that may impact your financial standing.

3. *Your experience with loans*. Basically, the lender wants to know that you are trustworthy and will hold up your end of the loan agreement. This means you need to be reliable and make good business decisions.

4. *Current holdings and financial situation*. Lenders are most interested in liquidity – your cash flow and income.

When lenders are looking at your ability to make a profit, they'll want to know about your total expenses related to the property. How much will it cost you to take care of the property? What will your insurance rates, taxes, and cost of repairs be? The lender wants to see that you can cover your costs associated with home ownership, as well as their interest charges.

Lenders often want short repayment periods, while it usually more beneficial for the buyer to have longer periods. Longer repayment periods mean that you can avoid origination fees, additional appraisal fees, and other costs. When it comes to loans for investment property, a 20 year fixed rate loan is considered a long loan. Normally this includes a balloon payment five to ten years into the loan.

If your lender tries to push you into a shorter repayment period, you can set up an arrangement that you re-price after five years, instead of having to pay a large amount of cash in one lump sum. A common alternative is the prevailing prime interest rate plus 1%.

Keep in mind that most things in real estate investing are negotiable, and that your lender can be your partner in real estate investing. Developing a positive long-term working relationship with your lender can only help you.

Hunting for Your Hidden Gem

Even in a strong market with the new technology available to give up-to-the- minute assessments of properties, an investor can lose large amounts of money in a short period of time. For the best chance to successful obtain your perfect investment property, consider these suggestions:

❑ Take advantage of the internet. You can find a "hidden gem" by searching through the millions of properties listed online, and viewing the property's description, pictures, asking price, and legal information. Usually, the only way to avoid a real estate agent fee is to look for property listed For Sale by Owner, or posted on other free sites.

❑ Look into getting your own access to the Multiple Listing Service (MLS). A license is required in some areas, but some places you can buy into the service for a fee.

❑ Get out and investigate the area that you're considering buying in person. Will the price be held down because of the condition of the neighborhood?

❑ If possible, talk to the neighbors. They might give up information about the property that the seller hasn't mention, like the front yard that floods after two days of rain.

❑ Get a professional inspection. When you make your offer, add a satisfactory home inspection contingency. Use a trusted professional inspector and carefully review the detailed inspection report. Few properties, even new construction, are perfect. Use the report to negotiate the repair of problems or an adjustment to the selling price.

The Importance of the Home Inspection

The condition of real estate is different in every situation. To protect yourself when making such a substantial investment, it is important to have a thorough inspection by a trained professional. Make your offer to purchase property contingent on a satisfactory home inspection, and you will avoid investing in a money pit.

What exactly is considered "satisfactory"? Any home containing wood should have a pest inspection, where the inspector looks for evidence of damage caused by termites, mice, carpenter ants or other pests. This inspection is separate from that done by the home inspector.

Your home inspector should focus on every mechanical and structural aspect of the property. They will look for substantial cracks in the foundation, levelness of the structure, and moisture in the basement. Water penetration is evident when there is mold, mildew or efflorescence - a white powder that shows where water has penetrated. High tech inspectors use lasers to see if the things are level and specialized radon gas meters to determine if there is a radon gas issue.

The structure of the home is closely inspected. Homes rest on top of a foundation. Floors have been installed on top of this foundation, and it needs to be inspected to ensure that proper materials have been used. Next, the walls might have improper framing or possible damage from water. Electrical and plumbing systems lie within the walls, and where possible, these interior systems are inspected for wear, out-of-code construction, and damage. Pipes are inspected for leaks or chemical concerns such as lead or rust. Some home inspectors test the water pressure and flow rate of the house.

The home's electrical system is completely inspected. The inspector looks for uncovered switches or outlets, incorrect wiring, insufficient grounding, faulty circuit breakers, or unsatisfactory GFCI trips.

Once in the attic, the inspector should check for water damage and air leaks. The framing is looked at to ensure that it is strong. The underside of the roof is inspected for a good seal where vent pipes go through the roof.

On the roof, the inspector examines it for holes, loose shingles or tile, poor flashing, or any other concern that might cause the roof to not hold up against the elements.

Heating and air-conditioning systems are inspected for adequate flow, duct leaks, and filter condition. Outdoor faucets are tested to be sure they work and don't leak or have inadequate water flow.

All appliances included with the sale of the house are examined. The hot water heater, stove, wood stoves and any other built-in units are check for proper function and standards compliance.

All of this information is compiled in the comprehensive inspection report that is available to the individual or company that paid for the inspection. Inspections benefit the buyer because they can use issues with the property as bargaining chips during negotiations. The home inspection is also beneficial to the seller because they then get an honest assessment of the condition of their property and can make improvements to some items before putting their home up for sale.

The home inspection is one area where a few hundred dollars spent often saves thousands of dollars during the purchase process.

Minimize your Risk with Insurance

In 2005, the median home price rose almost 15% over the previous year, and even more in some real estate markets. The minimum required FICO (credit score) was lowered, some of the documentation requirements were reduced, and the allowance for debt was increased to 45% of income. It is estimated that 30% of all new mortgages are interest-only mortgages. Almost 35% of home loans are Adjustable Rate Mortgages (ARMs). Starting in June 2004, the Federal Reserve has raised interest rates 11 times.

These stats indicate that there has been incredible growth in the real estate market over recent years. As the home prices have risen, so has the associate risk involved with buying and selling property. Thankfully, every type of risk now has an appropriate insurance. Of them all, the two most popular are title and liability insurance.

Title insurance ensures the coverage of any potential financial loss that is a result of an error in the processing and researching of a property title. Any lapses that might happen during the title search process, prior to closing, are covered. The title company will search a public record database to make sure that the property is able to be sold, meaning it's free of encumbrances. Public records are not always completely accurate, and errors can occur.

Liability insurance covers injuries that happen on, or because of, the property. If someone slips and falls on your property, your liability insurance would provide coverage. The more coverage you have, the more expensive it becomes.

Hazard insurance is available for less likely risks such as hurricanes, flooding, or earthquakes.

You can also get coverage for accidents created by humans. This includes chemical spills, electrical malfunctions, vandalism, theft, etc.

It's best to shop around for favorable rates, and pay close attention to your deductible amount, and any limitations on the policy.

Fixing the Property Reaps Financial Rewards

The best way to increase the likelihood that you'd get top dollar for your property is to fix it up. You do not have to be a trainer plumber or carpenter to make your home more attractive to buyers. With just a few tools and some hard work you can give your property a well-maintained appearance.

It's a good idea to go through the house and make minor repairs before showing it, or putting it on the market. A home inspection will likely be done before the final deal, so if you take the time up front to make the minor repairs, you'll be able to avoid some of the potential buyer's bargaining chips in negotiating a deal. Fix the leaky bathroom faucet and fix broken windows.

Take care of your property's curb appeal. Maintain the landscaping by trimming the lawn and shrubs, and planting some flowers. The outside of the home is what will draw in prospective buyers, or keep them driving.

Ask your neighbors to clean up their yard; offer to take their trash and junk away for them, ask them to move kid's toys, or offer to mow the lawns next to your property. You could even consider giving a small cash incentive after the successful sale of the home.

Your home should be super clean before you show it. It's usually too expensive to replace all the carpeting in a home, but getting it cleaned is affordable. Place your furniture in ways that mask worn spots. Put down new welcome mats and replace worn area rugs. Wash all the windows until they sparkle. Repair worn conduit, and replace air filters on air-conditioning and heating for a fresh look. Give the walls a fresh coat of paint.

Be sure the work looks professionally done, so that people can see the quality of your property. A well-maintained home usually garners a higher sales price than a home that has been neglected.

Selling it Yourself, or Use an Agent?

Selling your home yourself, also called FSBO or For Sale by Owner, is a realistic option thanks to the internet. People sell their own property without an agent because they avoid costly real estate agent commissions. This commission is typically about 6% of the property sale price. Agents work hard for their commissions, and provide valuable insight into the market and sales process.

They usually have valuable experience selling other properties in the area. If you sell it yourself, you stand to save thousands of dollars, but you are taking on all the work that the real estate agent does. Is selling your property FSBO right for you? Think about these points when making this decision:

❑ Pricing it right the first time. To price your property correctly, you need to know the market. A poor pricing decision can cost you - under pricing will result in lost potential earnings, and over pricing will cause the home to sit on the market while you are paying expensive carrying costs. Home prices vary depending on the square footage, lot size, age, and other factors. Use neighborhood comparables to judge the most appropriate list price.

❑ Get the word out. If you sell FSBO, you won't have access to the largest, most valuable marketing tool, the MLS. But thanks to the internet, the MLS isn't the only way to market your home. Put out signs, list it on websites, and place ads in the newspaper to let buyers know about your house.

❑ Can you negotiate successfully? Some people are born with this skill, and other have to work at it. If you are not a seasoned real estate negotiator, research the subject and learn enough about it to avoid losing money.

❑ Be a fast learner. You'll need to do what an agent does. Learn about the sales process, legal issues, contracts, closing process, insurance, and many other aspects of the selling real estate.

❑ Patience is important. Selling FSBO is a lot of work and small details, and you are in charge of managing them in order to get the job done.

Making the decision to do it yourself can be rewarding and save a lot of money, but a half-hearted attempted will most likely be unsuccessful.

Marketing Plan Development and Execution

Like it or not, you usually need to spend time marketing your property in order for it to sell. What is marketing? Marketing is the creation of a strategy used to sell an item. Research, promotion, advertising and sales are all part of marketing.

Research your local market, and the prices at which comparables sell. You'll need to have your finger on the pulse of the market during the entire sales process, which can take months. This is important because you may be in negotiations over a long period of time, and knowing the up-to-the-minute standing of your property will help you make educated negotiation decisions.

Advertising is needed to pull together a large group of interested buyers. By having many parties that want to purchase your property you may be able to create a bidding war which will drive up the sale price. How should you advertise? Use all of your advertising resources, like the newspaper, word-of-mouth, flyers, targeted mailings, special trade booklets, and the internet.

The internet is one of the most effective ways to market. There are many real estate investment websites that allow you to post your property with pictures. A comprehensive marketing campaign includes these online marketing tools. Find a site with good traffic and include flattering photos of the interior and exterior of your property. You can consider adding a virtual tour.

If It's Not Selling Quickly Enough

Real estate markets go through cycles. Depending where in the cycle you are, you may find it easy, or difficult, to sell your investment property. If the market has hit a plateau or gone down, you might have to wait for buyers. This will tie up money and make you have to wait to make a profit, which can be frustrating.

There are a few strategies you can use to get yourself out of this type of situation.

1. If it's your primary residence and you can afford to do so, wait it out. The market typically changes every 1 to 5 years, and you can sell on the next upswing.

2. Look at your property from the point-of-view of the buyer and make all necessary improvements. This will make your property more attractive to buyers. Think of what might be a deterrent and account for it. For example, if you live next to a loud highway, close the windows and play soft music to take away from this drawback.

3. Stage the house. Set out a few bouquets of flowers, turn the lights on, put on some light background music, bake some fresh cookies for a homey smell and welcomed snacks for visitors. Put out a flyer on the property with plenty of attractive

pictures, a reminder of the property highlights and your contact information. Make it so the buyer can see themselves living there. Buyers want a home they that makes them proud.

4. Encourage your neighbors to help you improve the appearance of the neighborhood.

5. Make sure you've priced the home correctly. Markets shift frequently, so you might not be priced competitively priced for the current market.

If you've tried these tips and the property has still not sold, try taking it off the market for awhile, and then list it again after re-checking your pricing. When houses sit on the market too long, potential buyers assume there must be something wrong. Extensively advertise your property. Making the extra effort to get your house sold will only help you make a profit.

Negotiating a Win-Win Deal

When negotiating, arm yourself with information and knowledge and you will be well equipped to broker a fair deal. Find out as much as you can about real estate law, the current market, and the other person's situation. If you are buying the house find out why they are selling. Are they in foreclosure? Has something happened personally that makes them eager to get rid of the property at any reasonable price? Find out how long the place has been on the market, the number of other offers, if any, and at what amount. Is there outstanding debt on the home, and if so how much? Are they up-to-date with their payments?

Most sellers won't just give out this information. Try to determine their status by giving up a bit of your own information first. Be careful about what you say because the seller might be able to use it when negotiating with you later.

When you are engaged with the other party in negotiating a contract, you're trying to come to a mutual agreement on the price of the property and terms. Consider the area comps, true condition of the property from the inspection report, and seller's situation. Before getting involved in any negotiation have your financing in place by being pre-approved. Before signing any written offers or contracts, seek legal counsel.

TIP: Make your offer in a non-round number. An offer of $233,200 vs. $230,000 might catch the seller off guard and leave them curious about what information you have that they don't.

CHAPTER 3

OTHER CONSIDERATIONS IN INVESTING

Know the Real Estate Law

Every part of real estate involves the law. There are many complicated legal pieces and many different people are involved in any real estate transaction.

First and foremost, the contract is most important part of buying and selling property. The primary purpose of a contract is to show mutual assent – the agreement by both parties to the exchange- in writing. Verbal agreements are not binding. To be valid a contract, it must include the following:

❑ Identification of the parties involved and the agreed upon price

❑ Specific "consideration" must be stated – something of value that's being exchanged, usually money

❑ Signatures of each party involved

There are checks-and-balances to protect people in every situation and to protect the overall system. Appraisals are used to ensure that the property is worth what the lender and seller have purported. The appraisal prevents shady deals being stuck between investors and mortgage brokers. Commercial property has its own laws regarding use and sale. If there are tenants living in the property, there are specific laws to protect the landlord and tenants. Lenders are held to the law by how much they can loan, what documents and insurance are required, and even how they market their financing programs.

It's important to know about tax law, or get advice from a professional, since it greatly impacts your success in real estate investing. Mistakes are costly, and by protecting yourself you can make decisions that will help your bottom line rather than take away your profits.

Investing Tax Implications

Before covering the subject of real estate tax law, understand that the following should not be thought of as legal advice. Seek legal advice from your attorney or accountant when making any legal or tax decisions.

Each area has its own tax codes, but here are a few general tips to consider that apply in most locations:

❑ You can sell your primary residence tax-free if you've lived there for two or more years. Investment property that's been sold is subject to capital gains tax, and if held for less than one year, it's at the regular income tax rates which can be as high as 35%. If the property is held one year or more before selling, it's considered a long term capital gain and is typically taxed at 15%.

❑ You can also sell tax-free if you keep the property as a residence for 730 days, not necessarily in a row. If you sell and reinvest the cash into a home of equal or greater value, you won't need to pay tax.

❑ "Like kind" investment trades, also known as the 1031 exchange, can be used to defer taxes. You can use this to trade undeveloped land for property with a house, a rental home for a commercial building, etc. You can take 45 days to locate up to 3 substitute properties, and you must have the closing within 180 days. You also need to retain a facilitator, or neutral party, to keep accurate records and hold the money. You cannot do a 1031 exchange with your primary residence.

❑ Mortgage interest can be deducted from your taxes. Loans valued at up to $1 million are eligible, and origination fees and points can be included.

Since the tax law is so complicated, it's best to seek professional assistance anytime you are in a situation that's out of the ordinary. The amount you pay for their services will be saved tenfold by their expertise in the field.

The Pros and Cons of Rural vs. Urban Investments

One real estate trend is the shift of buyers from populated urban locations to less populated rural places. Unique properties like vineyards, Bed & Breakfasts, horse farms, and agricultural farms, have realized increased property values thanks in part to aging, financially secure, baby boomers. Although these locations are desirable when investing in real estate, there are some challenges associated with rural properties.

Finding a property can be a challenge. With the increased popularity of people working from home, and more retirees looking for rural retreats, it can be difficult to find an investment property at a bargain price.

Finding reliable and qualified contractors that are affordable often presents a challenge in rural locations. You may need to pay a premium for skilled labor, even if the average income in the area is lower than in the city.

When property is unique, it's difficult to appraise. Many rural properties don't have realistic comps, so the value is essentially guessed. Lenders are aware of this type of situation, so they might to be less willing to finance a loan for a one- of-a-kind property. This usually isn't a problem if the buyer has solid credit and can provide a more substantial down payment.

When it comes time to sell a rural investment property, you will need to market your property over a larger area to pull together a group of interested, and qualified, potential buyers.

Investing in Real Estate Foreclosures

While some foreclosures may look appealing to the real estate investor, it's essential to consider many factors before you enter into a deal involving a foreclosed property.

What is foreclosure? It's a legal process that occurs when a mortgage holder takes back a property when payments are not current.

By buying a foreclosed property, you are entering into a legal mess. Some foreclosure situations allow for the 'right of redemption'. This means that the property owner can make back payments and take back the title. Obviously, you want to stay away from this. When considering a foreclosure, look for situations where, at minimum, a Notice of Default has been given.

A unique point about foreclosures is that the property is sold "as is". There are no warranties and no title insurance. Have a professional inspection beforehand, and never make an offer without looking at the property personally. If there are problems with the property but you are looking for a house to fix, reduce your offer appropriately. Before buying, conduct a thorough title search.

Two other types of foreclosure are REO and 'short sale' deals. REO stands for "real estate owned". This is when the lender owns the property because it was auctioned, but no one bought it. You can find a REO bargain, but be very careful. The property usually wasn't bought for a reason. Short sale deals happen when a lender will take less money than remains on the existing loan.

Investing in Commercial Property

Commercial real estate investment (CREI) accounts for a fraction of all real estate investments, with residential property being the largest segment. Just because it is a small piece of the pie doesn't mean it's less complicated.

Commercial property is most often bought for business purposes as an investment. Even if it's an apartment building with several apartments, it's considered commercial.

When investing in commercial property, you have to invest more money, which requires excellent credit. By putting more money down, you have exposed yourself to greater risk. Commercial investors also need to determine their capitalization rate (cap rate) and Gross Rent Multiplier (GRM) to decide if an investment is a good decision.

The cap rate and GRM are useful calculations when investing. The cap rate formula is: Annual Net Operating Income/Purchase Price. Usually, a sound investment has an 8-10% cap rate. The lower the percentage, the higher the risk and the lower the anticipated profit. The formula used to calculate the GRM is: Purchase Price/Monthly Gross Operating Income.

You should also consider the property comps, appraisal vs. assessment, income and replacement costs when considering if a deal is worth it.

Commercial properties are also tricky because the economic conditions of an area often dictate the occupancy of commercial property.

When buying commercial property, you'll need to first educate yourself on area zoning, leasing rules, commercial law, building maintenance, and other legal issues. Since the property will most likely be rented, you'll need to consider fire safety, internet and telephone capabilities, more complex plumbing and electrical needs, security systems, and more. Only when a landlord has a triple-net lease – where the tenant pays for and coordinates all maintenance, repairs, and insurance- will the involvement be less.

Of course a profit can be made from CREI. Although there are more risks, the potential profit is often higher.

The Pros and Cons of Renting Property

Sometimes investors hold onto property with the hopes of making a profit through rental, while benefiting from the capital appreciation and beneficial tax code.

When deciding whether to hold or sell a property, calculate out your estimated taxes if you keep the property, versus selling it. Hypothesize about future sales prices are going based on interest rates, trends, and the current market.

If you've decided to become a landlord, keep the following in mind:

1. Have all applicants complete an application. Use this information to conduct a complete background check; review rental and credit history, and talk to their references, previous landlords and employers.

2. Use a contract that's easy to understand and is fair. It should include information about the amount and stipulations of the deposit, under what conditions and how much notice is needed for the landlord to enter the rental, who is responsible for what, etc.

3. Do what you say, and more. Keep your tenants happy and chances are they'll pay the rent. If you're slow to respond to maintenance requests or don't keep up the property, they might stop paying rent.

4. If a tenant is late with the rent, find out why right away. Encourage them to have the rent paid by the due date by reminding them of the late fee clause in the lease. Keep clear records of payments because you may need this information if legal action were ever required.

5. If you do need to take legal action, try to first go through arbitration. Cases are typically handled faster and more efficiently.

Alternative Real Estate Investment Instruments

There are ways to invest in real estate without ever having to deal with the nitty gritty parts of the business – no inspection, appraisal, or marketing. Real Estate Financial Trusts (REITs), Mortgage-Backed Securities (MBS), and Self-Directed IRAs are all ways of investing in real estate on paper alone.

Real Estate Financial Trusts (REITs) are mutual funds that focus on real estate; investments are made in both physical property and mortgage portfolios. It's handled like other securities and has special tax situations. REITs often have better yields and provide easier access to cash than traditional property investment.

There are Mortgage, Equity, and Hybrid REITs. Mortgage REITs invest in mortgages, with revenue coming from the mortgage interest. Equity REITs own and invest in actual real estate, with most of the revenue coming from rental income. Hybrid REITs are a combination of both.

Just like other mutual funds, once purchased they can't be cashed in through the fund, but have to be sold to another investor through a broker.

REITs can be considered high yield, since dividends are paid out to shareholders at 90% or more of taxable earnings. Dividends plus appreciation equals the total return, and REITs are comparable to small-cap stock in that about 66% of the return comes from the dividends. As a result, REITs are impacted by changes in interest rates. When interest rates increase, the price of REITs usually decline.

Mortgage-Back Securities are bonds backed by a group of mortgage loans. Just like other type of bonds, you earn a coupon rate of interest. Unlike other bonds, however, investors get repayments of the principle in small parts, over the duration of the MBS, as the mortgage loans that back the MBS are paid off, instead of in one lump sum when the security matures.

One of the reasons that the MBS is a stable investment is because there are so many loans in the pool; the few loans that default or pay off early do not eliminate the investor's profit.

When choosing between closed MBS and pre-payable MBS, determine if interest rates are likely to rise or fall. Mortgage holders can pre-pay their mortgages, and if interest rates drop people will refinance to take advantage of better rates, both scenarios will negatively impact the MBS investor. If interest rates are expected to drop, a closed MBS is the better option.

A Self-Directed Individual Retirement Account (IRA) can hold assets such as land, single family residences, and commercial property instead of just cash.

Before you invest in any real estate investment, contact a financial professional and do your own research to make the best decision for you.

CONCLUSION

Real estate is a multi-faceted, multi-billion dollar industry. As an investor, it's important to know the business and take some calculated risks in order to turn a profit. From each investment experience you will gain valuable skills that you can apply to future investing endeavors.

Printed by Libri Plureos GmbH in Hamburg, Germany

9 786069 836880